1 Introduction

The unique characteristics of animals is a miscellany of facts, genuine or supposed, gleamed from earlier and contemporary Greek writers (No Latin writer is once named) and to a limited extent from his own observation to illustrate the habits of the animal world.

We are of course prepared to encounter much that modern science rejects, but the general tone with its search after the picturesque, the startling, even the miraculous, would justify us in ranking Aelian with the paradoxical, rather than with the sober exponents of natural history.

Mythology, mariners' yarns, vulgar superstitions, the ascertained facts of nature — all serve to adorn a tale and, on occasion, to point a moral. His religion is the popular stoicism of the age. Aleian repeatedly affirms his belief in the gods and in divine providence; the wisdom and beneficence of Nature are held up to veneration; the folly and selfishness of man are contrasted with the untaught virtues of the animal world. Some animals, to be sure, have their failings, but he chooses rather to dwell upon their good qualities, devotion, courage, self-sacrifice, gratitude. Again, animals are guided by reason, and from them we may learn contentment, control of the passions, and calm in the face of death.

His primary object is to entertain and while so doing to convey instruction in the most agreeable form. Some might find fault with his random and piece-meal handling of his theme-of which he is well aware, and he defends himself with the plea that a frequent change of topic helps to maintain the reader's interest and saves him from boredom.

As to the permanent value of his work he has no misgivings and since we have been informed that his writings were much admired, we may assume that they appealed to cultivated circles in a way that the voluminous and possibly arid compilations of grammarians did not.

Now I am well aware of the labour that others have expended on this subject, yet I have collected all the materials that I could; I have clothed them in untechnical language, and am persuaded that my achievement is a treasure far from negligible. So if anyone considers them profitable, let him make use of them; anyone who does not consider them so may give them to his father to keep and attend to.

Animal Peculiarity Part 6

By T.P Just

~~~

Copyright © 2010 by Terence Just. All rights reserved.

Animal Peculiarity Part 1
Animal Peculiarity Part 2
Animal Peculiarity Part 3
Animal Peculiarity Part 4
Animal Peculiarity Part 5
Animal Peculiarity Part 6
Animal Peculiarity Part 7
Animal Peculiarity Part 8
Just Enterprises

Table of Contents

2 The Ibis

Here is another story relating to the Egyptian Ibis which I
have heard. The bird is sacred to the moon. At any rate it
hatches its eggs in the same number of days that the goddess
takes to Wax and to wane, and never leaves Egypt.
The reason for this is that Egypt is the moistest of all countries
and the moon is believed to be the moistest of all planets.
Of its own free will the Ibis would never quit Egypt, and
should some man lay hands upon it and forcibly export it, it
will defend itself against its assailant and bring all his labour
to nothing, for it will starve itself to death and render its
captor's exertions vain.
It walks quietly like a maiden, and one would never see it
moving at anything faster than a foot's pace. The Black Ibis
does not permit the winged serpents from Arabia to cross into
Egypt, but fights to protect the land it loves, while the other
kind encounters the serpents that come down the Nile when
in flood and destroys them.
Otherwise there would have been nothing to prevent the
Egyptians from being killed by their coming.

3 The Golden Eagle

There is, I am told, a species of eagle to which men have given the name of 'Golden Eagle,' though others call it Asterias (starred). And it is seldom seen. Aristotle says that it hunts fawns, hares, cranes, and geese of the farmyard.

It is believed to be the largest of eagles; at any rate men say that it attacks bulls with violence, and its method of attack they describe as follows.

Its method of attacking bulls

The bull is feeding with his head down, and the Eagle alights upon his neck and with its beak delivers a rain of powerful blows. And the bull goes Wild as though stung by a gadfly, and sets off to run as fast as he can go.

So long as the land makes going easy the Eagle bides its time, flying above him and Watching. But directly it sees the bull near a precipice it makes an arch with its wings, covers the bull's eyes so that he cannot see what is before him, and down he goes with a fearful crash.

Whereupon the Eagle pounces, rips open his stomach, 'and has no difficulty in enjoying its prey to its heart's content. But the prey killed by some other creature it will not touch: rather it delights in its own labours and will not for one moment admit any other creature to share them.

Later when it has gorged itself, it breathes over the rest of the carcase a foul and most ill-smelling air, leaving the remains unfit for any other animal to eat.

What is more, Eagles -build their nests far apart from one another so as to avoid quarrelling over their prey [and being a constant source of mutual hurt].

The Eagle, its devotion to its keeper

It seems that Eagles are full of affection even towards their keepers; Witness the Eagle that belonged to Pyrrhus, which (they say) on the death of its master abstained from food and died too.

And there was once an Eagle reared by a private citizen which -threw itself on to the pyre where its master's body was burning. Some say that it had been reared not by a man but by a Woman.

And to its young

The Eagle is apparently the most jealous guardian of its young. At any rate if it sees anyone approaching them, it does not allow him to depart unpunished, for it beats him with its Wings and lacerates him with its talons; and the punishment it inflicts is moderate, for it does not use its beak.

4 The Red Mullet

The Red Mullet is of all sea animals the most gluttonous and indisputably the most unrestrained in tasting everything it comes across.

And some of them are known as 'roughs,' deriving their name from places where there are rough rocks full of holes and thick growths of seaweed in them, and where there is a bottom of mud or sand.

A Red Mullet would eat the dead body of a man or of a fish, and its special delight is in filthy, ill-smelling food.

5 The Falcon

Falcons are excellent at fowling and are no whit inferior to eagles; they are by nature the tamest "of birds and the most attached to man; in size they a are as large as eagles. And I am told that in Thrace they even join with men in the pursuit of marsh-fowl.

And this is how they do it. The men spread their nets -and keep still while the Falcons fly over them and scare the fowl and drive them into the circle of nets. For this the Thracians allot a portion of their catch to the Falcons and find them trusty friends; if they do not do so, they at once deprive themselves of helpers.

Now the full-grown Falcon will fight both with a fox and with an eagle; with a vulture it frequently fights. But a Falcon will never eat the heart, thereby presumably fulfilling some mystic rite. If a Falcon sees the dead body of a man (so it is said), it always heaps earth upon the unburied corpse, though Solon laid no such injunction upon it, and will never touch the body.

And it even refrains from drinking if a solitary man is engaged in leading off -water into a channel, feeling sure that it will cause damage to the man who so labours if it purloins the water which he needs.

But if several men are engaged in irrigating, it sees that the stream is abundant and takes its share from the loving-cup, so to speak, which they offer, and is glad to drink.

6 The Kestrel, the Orites Hawk

There is a species of hawk known as the Kestrel which has no need whatever to drink. Another species is the Orites Hawk. Both species are remark- ably addicted to the female bird and pursue it after the manner of lovesick men and never cease from the pursuit.

But should the female chance to disappear without the male noticing it, he is overcome with grief and cries aloud and is like one in the depths of woe from love.

7 Hawks of Egypt

At the beginning of spring the Hawks of Egypt select two from all their number and dispatch them to reconnoitre certain desert islands off the coast of Libya. When they return they act as leaders to the rest in their flight.

And their arrival is the occasion of rejoicing on the part of the Libyans at their sojourn, for they do no damage whatever. And having reached the islands which the original scouts decided were the most suitable for them, they there lay and hatch their eggs in complete security and peace; and they hunt sparrows and pigeons and rear their young in an abundance of food.

Then when these have grown strong and are able to fly, they take the young' birds with them back to Egypt as though they were going to their own homes, that is to their haunts in regions they have grown to know.

The Hawk and eye-troubles

When Hawks are troubled with their eyesight they go straight to some stone wall and pull up some Wild lettuce and then holding it above their eyes allow the bitter, astringent juice to drip in; and this restores their health.

And men say that doctors use this drug for the benefit of those whose sight is affected, and the remedy derives its name from these birds. And men do not refuse to be called the disciples of birds; rather they admit as much.

Hawk reveals sacrilege

It is said that once upon a time a Hawk at Delphi proved a man guilty of sacrilege by swooping upon him and striking his head. It is also believed that Hawks are bastards, if they be compared with the various kinds of eagles.

8 The Rainbow Wrasses

Rainbow Wrasses are nurslings of rocks and their mouth is full of poison, and whatever fish they touch they render uneatable.

Indeed if it should happen that fishermen, coming upon a half-eaten prawn and fancying that their catch is unsalable, should taste it, they are assailed by convulsions and torments in their stomach.

And the Wrasses also molest those who dive and swim in pursuit of fish, falling upon them in great numbers and biting them, exactly like flies on land; so that one must either beat them off or be tormented by being eaten up. But while one is busy beating them off, there is no time to attend to one's work.

9 The Sea-hare

The Sea-hare when eaten has often been the cause even of
death; in any case it causes pains in the stomach.
It is born in the mud and is not infrequently caught along with
sprats. In appearance it is not unlike a snail without its shell.

10 All Vultures are female

It is said that no male Vulture is ever born: all Vultures are female. And the birds knowing this and fearing to be left childless, take measures to pro- duce them as follows.
They fly against the south wind. If however the wind is not from the south, they open their beaks to the east wind, and the in- rush of air impregnates them, and their period of gestation lasts for three years. But the Vulture is said never to make a nest.

The 'Aegypius'

The Aegypius however, which is on the border line between the vulture and the eagle, is both male and female, and is black in colour, and I am told that their nests are pointed out, But I have been informed that Vultures do not lay eggs, but that in their birth-pangs they produce chicks, and that these are feathered from birth have also heard.

The Kite

There is no limit to the robberies of the Kite. If they can manage pieces of meat on sale in the market, they pounce upon them and carry them off; on the other hand they will not touch sacrifices offered to Zeus. But the Mountain Kite pounces upon birds and peeks out their eyes.

11 The Ravens in Egypt

The Ravens in Egypt which live beside the Nile at first appear to be begging of the people sailing on the river, soliciting to be given something.

And if they are given, they stop begging; but if their solicitations fail, they fly in a mass and perch on the sail yards of the ship and proceed to eat the ropes and to cut the cords.

The Raven in Libya

But the Ravens of Libya, when men through fear of thirst draw water and fill their vessels and place them on the roof so that the fresh air may keep the water from putrefying, the Ravens, I say, help themselves to drink by bending over and inserting their beaks as far as they will go.

And when the water gets too low they gather pebbles in their mouth and claws and drop them into the earthen ware vessel. Now the pebbles are borne down by their weight and sink, while the water owing to their pressure rises.

So the Ravens by a most ingenious contrivance get their drink; they know by some mysterious instinct that one space will not contain two bodies.

The Raven

Aristotle asserts that Ravens know the difference between a prosperous and a barren country, and in one that produces all things in plenty they move about in flocks and great numbers, but in a barren and unfruitful country in pairs.

As to their young ones, when fully grown, every Raven banishes them from its nest. For that reason they seek their food (for themselves) and neglect to care for their parents.

12 Poisonous Fishes

Among fishes the Goby, the Weever, and the Flying Gurnard emit poison when they prick one; not that they are deadly; whereas the Sting-ray with its barb kills on the spot.

A Sting-ray

And Leonidas of Byzantium tells how a man who knew nothing of fishes and could not distinguish them, stole a Sting-ray from a fishing-net the poor fellow must have taken it for a flounder-, took it and put it in his bosom and walked off as though he had found something good, some spoil whose sale would be profitable to him.

But the Sting-ray hurt by the pressure, struck and pierced him with its sting, causing the wretched thief's bowels to gush out. And there the thief lay dead beside the Sting-ray, clear evidence of what he had done in his ignorance.

13 The Raven, its daring

Of the Raven you might say that it has a spirit no less daring than the eagle, for it even attacks animals, and not the smallest either, but asses and bulls. It settles on their neck and peeks them, and in many cases it actually gouges out their eyes. And it fights with that vigorous bird the Merlin and whenever it sees it fighting with a fox, it comes to the fox's rescue, for it is on friendly terms with the animal.

Its various tones

The Raven must really be the most clamorous of birds and have the largest variety of tones, for it can be taught to speak like a human being. For playful moods it has one voice, for serious moods another, and if it is delivering answers from the gods, then its voice assumes a devout and prophetic tone.

Its diet

Ravens know that in summer they suffer from looseness of the bowels; for that reason they are careful to abstain from moist food.

14 Viviparous Animals

Aristotle tells us that some animals are viviparous; others oviparous, that others again produce grubs.
The viviparous are man and all other creatures that have hair, and among marine animals the cetaceans.
And of these some have a blow-hole but no gills, like the dolphin and the whale.

15 Hornless Oxen of Moesia

In Moesia the Oxen draw loads and are hornless. And I maintain that it is not due to the cold that herds are to be seen without horns, but that it is due to the peculiar nature of the Oxen.

And the proof is to hand, for even in Scythia there are oxen not destitute of the glory of horns.

16 Bees in Scythia

And I have learnt from one who records the fact in his history that there are even Bees in Scythia and that they do not mind the cold at all. And what is more, the Scythians bring and sell to the Moesians honey, which is no alien produce but native, and honey- comb of their own country.

If I contradict Herodotus, I hope he will not be angry with me, for the man who reported these things vowed that he was presenting the results of his own enquiry and not merely repeating what he had heard and what we could not verify.

17 The Shark and its young

The Shark brings forth its young through its mouth in the sea and takes them back again and then disgorges them by the same channel alive and unharmed.

The Parrot Wrasse

I learn that of saltwater fishes the Parrot Wrasse alone regurgitates its food and eats it after-wards, as sheep do, which are said to chew the cud.

The mouse and its liver

The liver of the Mouse has the most astounding and unexpected habit of growing a lobe day by day as the moon waxes, up to the middle of the month. Then again in proportion as the month declines, so the lobe gradually dwindles until it loses its shape and disappears into the body.

A Shower of mice

And I am told that when it hails in the Thebaid, mice are to be seen on the earth, and one part of them is still mud while the other is already flesh.

Of Frogs

And I myself on a journey from Naples to Dicaearchia encountered a shower of frogs, and the forepart of them was crawling, supported by two feet, while the other part trailed behind, still formless, seeming to consist of some moist substance.

Get All The Books In The Series:

Animal Peculiarity Part 1
Animal Peculiarity Part 2
Animal Peculiarity Part 3
Animal Peculiarity Part 4
Animal Peculiarity Part 5
Animal Peculiarity Part 6
Animal Peculiarity Part 7
Animal Peculiarity Part 8

www.ingramcontent.com/pod-product-compliance
Lightning Source LLC
Chambersburg PA
CBHW050922290526

45792CB00002B/854